FOUNDATIONS OF OUR NATION

GEORGE WASHINGTON AND THE AMERICAN PRESIDENCY

by Michael Regan

FOCUS
READERS

WWW.FOCUSREADERS.COM

Focus Readers is distributed by North Star Editions:
sales@northstareditions.com | 888-417-0195

Produced for Focus Readers by Red Line Editorial.

Content Consultant: Dr. Gideon Mailer, Associate Professor of History, University of Minnesota Duluth

Photographs ©: Everett - Art/Shutterstock Images, cover, 1; North Wind Picture Archives, 4–5, 7, 9, 10–11, 15, 17, 21, 25, 29; Augustus Weidenbach/Library of Congress, 13; Everett Historical/Shutterstock Images, 18–19; Red Line Editorial, 27

ISBN
978-1-63517-248-5 (hardcover)
978-1-63517-313-0 (paperback)
978-1-63517-443-4 (ebook pdf)
978-1-63517-378-9 (hosted ebook)

Library of Congress Control Number: 2017935898

Printed in the United States of America
Mankato, MN
June, 2017

ABOUT THE AUTHOR

Michael Regan lives in southern Arizona with his spouse and two cats. He enjoys hiking, reading, tai chi, and going on adventures to new places.

TABLE OF CONTENTS

CHAPTER 1

Who Needs a President? 5

CHAPTER 2

The Executive Branch 11

VOICES FROM THE PAST

The First Political Parties 16

CHAPTER 3

Washington Shapes the Presidency 19

CHAPTER 4

The First President's Farewell 25

Focus on George Washington
and the American Presidency • 30
Glossary • 31
To Learn More • 32
Index • 32

WHO NEEDS A PRESIDENT?

The American colonies declared their independence from Great Britain in 1776. At this time, the colonies were not united. Each colony wanted to be free from British rule. But the colonies also wanted to run their own governments. The idea of a central US government was not popular.

Americans tore down statues of King George III after the colonies declared their independence.

By 1786, the American Revolutionary War (1775–1783) was over. The United States was officially independent. But the country was almost out of money. The states realized the country needed a stronger government. Some of the states called for a meeting. The people at the meeting wanted to create a constitution. This document would set the rules for a stronger central government.

The meeting resulted in heated debates. People made many difficult **compromises**. But finally, in September 1787, the US Constitution was signed. The document created three branches of government. The legislative branch,

Leaders met in Philadelphia, Pennsylvania, to write the US Constitution.

known as Congress, would make laws. The judicial branch would decide if laws failed to follow the Constitution. And the executive branch put the laws into effect. The president would be the leader of the executive branch.

The president would have a great deal of power. That made some people concerned. They were afraid of one person having too much power. They did not want the president to be a king. After all, the United States had gained independence from the king of Great Britain. Another king might lead to similar problems.

George Washington had been a military leader during the American Revolutionary War. His leadership made him a national hero. When it was time to select the first president, voters chose Washington. He won the election in 1789.

George Washington was sworn in as president on April 30, 1789.

Washington was now in charge of the executive branch. But he faced a major challenge. No other nation had a similar leader. That meant Washington did not have a model to follow. So, one of his most important jobs was to figure out what it meant to be a president.

CHAPTER 2

THE EXECUTIVE BRANCH

The main job of the executive branch is to make sure people follow the laws Congress creates. But the president has other jobs, too. For example, he or she is the leader of the military. That means the president is in charge of protecting the nation.

People had a celebration in New York City after President Washington was sworn in.

The president also has the power to approve the laws Congress creates. If the president does not like a law, he or she can **veto** it. The president can also suggest laws to Congress.

In addition, the president meets with other world leaders. He or she can make **treaties** with other countries. The president also chooses people to do important government jobs. These include judges and leaders of **agencies**.

That is a lot of work for one person. But the president does not do all of these jobs alone. A group known as the cabinet gives the president advice. Cabinet

George Washington vetoed two laws during his presidency.

members also run certain agencies in the government.

George Washington's cabinet had only four people. Thomas Jefferson was the secretary of state. His job involved meeting with leaders of other countries.

Alexander Hamilton was the secretary of the treasury. His job was to deal with matters relating to money. Henry Knox was the secretary of war. He was responsible for the military. Edmund Randolph was the attorney general. He was in charge of legal matters. Since Washington's time, the number of government agencies has grown. By the 2010s, the cabinet had 16 members.

The executive branch is powerful. But the Constitution has a system of checks and balances. That means the other two branches have power over the executive branch. For example, the judicial branch may decide the presidents' actions do

The members of George Washington's cabinet discussed ways to help the president.

not follow the Constitution. Also, the president must get permission from Congress for certain actions. These actions include going to war and creating treaties. Congress can also **override** a president's veto. That happens when two-thirds of Congress votes for a law. Then the president must uphold the law even if he or she does not like it.

THE FIRST POLITICAL PARTIES

In general, the writers of the Constitution did not like political parties. They believed political parties could divide the country. They also believed parties could lead to **corruption**. George Washington warned against political parties when he became president in 1789. He said he didn't want "separate views" to "misdirect" the country's leaders.

However, Washington had close ties to the nation's first political party. This group was known as the Federalists. They wanted a strong national government. The opposing party, the Anti-Federalists, wanted the government to leave states alone.

Alexander Hamilton was a Federalist. He wrote that all political parties had an "intolerant spirit."

Alexander Hamilton wrote many articles supporting the US Constitution and a strong central government.

He said some Anti-Federalist members were "wise and good men" and had "upright intentions." But their fear of losing personal liberty would actually decrease the security of the country.

Today, the two major political parties are the Democrats and the Republicans. They carry on this debate. Democrats tend to favor a strong national government. Republicans tend to want a small national government.

CHAPTER 3

WASHINGTON SHAPES THE PRESIDENCY

The Constitution gives the president control of the executive branch. But the Constitution does not describe those powers in detail. Washington knew he would be shaping the office for those who followed. His actions set a **precedent** for future presidents. In particular, four actions stood out.

George Washington was sworn in for his second term in 1793.

First, Washington showed the president's right to use the military. In 1791, a group of farmers refused to pay a new tax on alcohol. They beat up and shot at tax collectors. They even organized troops to fight against the government. This event became known as the Whiskey Rebellion. In 1794, Washington ordered the US Army to stop the revolt.

Second, Washington showed that the executive branch would carry out the laws Congress created. By stopping the Whiskey Rebellion, Washington was upholding a law on taxes. He made sure the tax collectors could do their job.

Farmers held tax collectors at gunpoint during the Whiskey Rebellion.

Third, Washington created the idea of executive privilege. This means the president can refuse to give information to the other two branches of government. In 1796, for example, Congress asked for papers related to a treaty.

Washington refused. He reminded Congress that the Constitution gave Congress no role in making treaties.

Fourth, Washington showed how long a president should serve. Each election allows the president to serve a four-year term. Washington was popular. He was elected to two terms. The Constitution did not set a limit on the number of terms a president could serve. Washington could have run for a third term. Instead, he chose to retire at the end of his second term. He did not want presidents to become like kings who served for life. Future presidents followed this precedent. They retired after two terms. However, that changed in the 1940s. Franklin D. Roosevelt was elected to a third and fourth term. In 1951, the Constitution was changed. It said a president could serve only two terms.

WHAT IF THE PRESIDENT DIES?

If the president dies while in office, the following people are next in line.

1 VICE PRESIDENT

2 SPEAKER OF THE HOUSE OF REPRESENTATIVES

3 PRESIDENT PRO TEMPORE OF THE SENATE

4 SECRETARY OF STATE

5 SECRETARY OF THE TREASURY

6 SECRETARY OF DEFENSE

7 ATTORNEY GENERAL

CHAPTER 4

THE FIRST PRESIDENT'S FAREWELL

Washington led the executive branch for eight years. He showed the nation what it meant to be president. But it was an exhausting job. By the end of his second term, he was ready to step down. Before leaving, Washington wrote his Farewell **Address**. In 1796, he laid out some of his most important beliefs.

After President Washington wrote his Farewell Address, it was printed in a newspaper.

He hoped his address would help guide the young nation.

Washington talked about the dangers of political parties. He also mentioned the need for a strong national government. He feared that disagreements between states could destroy the country. The nation would be stronger if the states were closely united, he said.

In addition, Washington warned against long-term **alliances** with other countries. He believed foreign countries would only look out for their own interests. They would not worry about the interests of the United States. So, Washington favored business agreements instead of alliances. These could be good for both nations, he said.

CAPITAL OF THE UNITED STATES

From 1790 to 1800, the US capital was Philadelphia. In 1800, the capital moved to the newly built District of Columbia. Leaders named the city Washington in honor of the first president.

THE UNITED STATES IN 1800

Philadelphia

Washington, DC

■ US STATES
☐ US TERRITORY

Washington also left an important topic out of his address. He did not mention slavery. Washington's feelings about the issue changed over time. When Washington was a boy, his father died. Washington inherited a farm and 10 enslaved people. At this time, Washington accepted slavery. Later in life, he decided not to buy or sell slaves. During the Revolutionary War, the idea of freedom took on new meaning to Washington. Slavery did not fit with this idea. Washington freed all his slaves when he and his wife died.

The debate over slavery continued for decades. In the 1860s, it nearly tore the

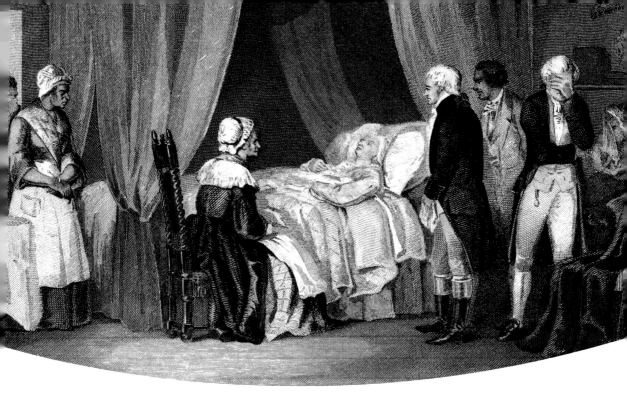

George Washington died at his home in Virginia on December 14, 1799.

country apart. Slavery was a major cause of the US Civil War (1861–1865).

Today, the executive branch continues to play an important role in the US government. It has served the citizens of the United States for more than 230 years.

FOCUS ON
GEORGE WASHINGTON AND THE AMERICAN PRESIDENCY

Write your answers on a separate piece of paper.

1. Write a short paragraph describing the main ideas of Chapter 3.

2. Do you think the United States needs a strong central government? Why or why not?

3. Who served as Washington's attorney general?
   - **A.** Thomas Jefferson
   - **B.** Edmund Randolph
   - **C.** Alexander Hamilton

4. Who does the president talk to when deciding how to carry out laws?
   - **A.** the cabinet
   - **B.** the judicial branch
   - **C.** the legislative branch

Answer key on page 32.

GLOSSARY

address
A formal speech or piece of writing.

agencies
Government departments that are responsible for a particular activity.

alliances
Groups of people or countries that join together.

compromises
Settlements of arguments in which both sides give in a little.

corruption
Dishonest or illegal acts, especially by powerful people.

override
To reject or cancel.

precedent
An earlier action that is used as a guide for later actions in a similar situation.

treaties
Official agreements that are made between two or more countries or groups.

veto
To reject a law made by Congress.

TO LEARN MORE

BOOKS

Britton, Tamara L. *George Washington*. Minneapolis: Abdo
  Publishing, 2017.
Caravantes, Peggy. *The American Revolution: 12 Things to
  Know*. North Mankato, MN: 12-Story Library, 2016.
Spalding, Maddie. *How the Executive Branch Works*.
  Mankato, MN: The Child's World, 2016.

NOTE TO EDUCATORS

Visit **www.focusreaders.com** to find lesson plans,
activities, links, and other resources related to this title.

INDEX

American
  Revolutionary War, 6,
  8, 28
Anti-Federalists, 16

cabinet, 12–14
Civil War, US, 29
Congress, 7, 11–12, 15,
  20–22
Constitution, 6–7,
  14–16, 19, 22–23

executive branch, 7, 9,
  11, 14, 19–20, 25, 29
executive privilege, 21

Farewell Address, 25
Federalists, 16

Great Britain, 5, 8

Hamilton, Alexander,
  14, 16

Jefferson, Thomas, 13
judicial branch, 7, 14

Knox, Henry, 14

Randolph, Edmund, 14

slavery, 28–29

Washington, George,
  8–9, 13–14, 17,
  19–22, 25–26, 28
Whiskey Rebellion, 20

Answer Key: **1.** Answers will vary; **2.** Answers will vary; **3.** B; **4.** A